attempts to show something of the unique charm of Belfast in an attractive and portable form. It looks at the positive atmosphere and life that is evident here, the energy, diversity and quality of a great city.

To see more of Chris Andrews work please go to :
www.cap-ox.com
and for more of the Gateway Publishing Ltd portfolio please see: **www.gatewaysark.co.uk**

A LITTLE SOUVENIR
Belfast

Chris Andrews

2 The Titanic Quarter and Belfast Lough

CLEARWAY
TITANIC
STUDIOS

Introduction

Belfast is the vibrant jewel in the crown of Northern Ireland. It is a self-confident city, full of opportunity and enjoying a unique and energetic renaissance. It is a place with a proud economic history, creative culture, passion and world-renowned friendliness. There is a lively pulse beating in the very heart of Belfast, a pulse which drives the city's rejuvenated business sector, eclectic tourist industry and burgeoning arts scene. Belfast's personality is evident within its historic buildings, famous pubs, café bars and rich cultural life. This is all manifested through a host of galleries, festivals and the now world-famous Titanic Quarter.

Small in size, Belfast is a compact metropolis with

The Crown

much to offer the businessman and tourist alike. It is a proud city encapsulated within majestic scenery, just waiting to be discovered and explored.

Belfast nestles between the imposing Divis and Black Mountains and the rolling Castlereagh Hills. To the north lies the spectacular and historic Cave Hill, where dramatic basalt cliffs sweep down to the shore of the Lough.

Belfast grew in importance throughout the seventeenth and eighteenth centuries and soon eclipsed its neighbour Carrickfergus in importance as a mercantile town. Throughout the nineteenth century, rapid

North Belfast with the Belfast Hills beyond

industrialisation transformed Belfast from a thriving town into a major city at the centre of the British Empire.

Extensive engineering projects eventually tamed the wide and meandering Lagan River and a port was established from which prosperity grew. Linen, engineering and – most famously – shipbuilding were the rocks on which Belfast's reputation and riches were founded. The Industrial Revolution left the city with a sense of civic and economic pride; it could boast, amongst other things, the world's largest shipyards and linen mills; tobacco and mineral water factories; and a ropeworks which dwarfed all others throughout the globe. Belfast soon replaced Dublin as Ireland's premier city and rivalled Glasgow, Liverpool and Manchester in size and importance.

Belfast has consistently transformed itself on the world stage and has cast off its long-held negative reputation to become a place of pride and a 'must-see' on the tourist trail. Visitors today find a thriving, pulsating and creative place which stands on the cusp of a truly golden era. It is a city that has flourished by looking to the future whilst taking, perhaps, a furtive glance over its shoulder at the past. It is a unique place, a legacy far removed from many pre-conceived perceptions.

Yet, there is more to Belfast than just the story of a vibrant city; it is also a tale of success arising from adversity. Since the mid-1990s, Belfast has thrived as an economic, cultural and tourist destination. CNN labelled Belfast one of Europe's 'hottest' destinations in 2013, additionally Lonely Planet has advised its readers to "get to Belfast before the rest of the world comes". The Financial Times has labelled the city as one of the Top 10 places in the world to hold a conference or a major event and the city's

The Spirit of Belfast sculpture and street entertainers in the city centre

 Replica of Titanic's bow in the dry dock and pump-house area

two airports have helped to make it one of the most visited weekend destinations in Europe.

On first impression, Belfast's greatness and grandeur may not be obvious, but scratch the surface and you will find it. The City is a place driven by re-invention, where character and resilience have yielded a dividend in tandem with peace. The pace of change may have been considerable, but it is also recognised that many challenges still have to be addressed if Belfast is to achieve its full potential as a world-acknowledged, popular and successful city.

This little book shows some of the charm and atmosphere that is here to be seen.

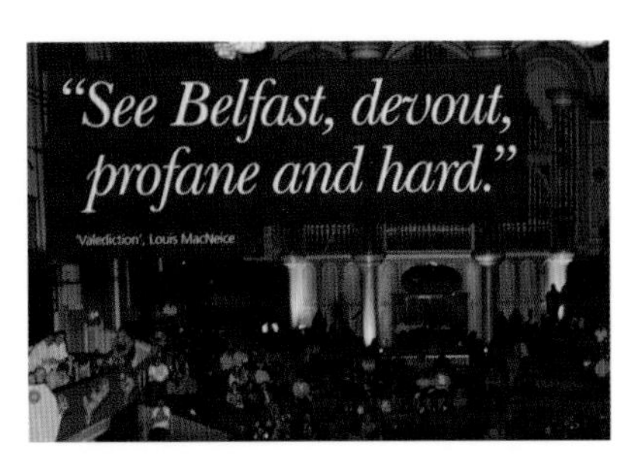

10 Developments along the River Lagan include the Queen's Bridge and Belfast Waterfront conference, arts and entertainment centre

The Lagan Weir and *Big Fish*

The Clarendon Graving Dock and pump-house (a graving dock is a dry dock used for maintainence of ships' hulls)

The Lagan waterfront and commemorative sculpture

14 Office buildings and a floating museum on the Lagan

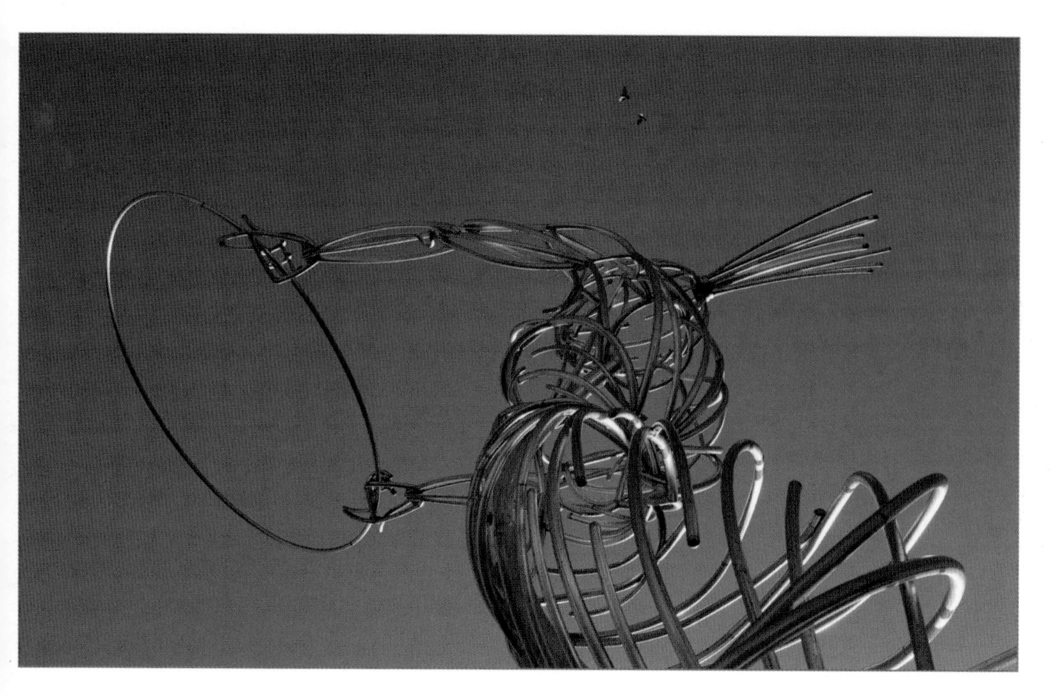

Harmony or *The Beacon of Hope* in Thanksgiving Square

 Belfast Botanic Gardens. The Palm House is one of the earliest glasshouses built in the world

 Relaxing in the grounds of City Hall

View into the city from Belfast Castle

The Castle Gardens and one of nine cat representations in the grounds

 The Royal Courts of Justice and Chichester Street

24 Docks and wind turbine construction

Titanic Studios, where *The Game of Thrones* is produced, formerly Harland and Wolff's paintshop

26 **Belfast Waterfront and offices along the Lagan**

NI Railways bridge over the river

 Titanic's slipway behind the Titanic Building and the old Harland and Wolff drawing offices

Wheel and compass of SS Nomadic, the only remaining White Star Line ship

SS Nomadic and the Titanic Building

 Original pump-house controls at the Titanic Dry Dock

The First World War cruiser HMS Caroline moored in the Titanic Quarter

34 View down the Lagan to the Lough

Ulster Hall, one of the oldest purpose-built concert halls in the British Isles

Belfast life and pub culture! Old advertising signs at The Duke of York and the interior of Kelly's Cellars

Bittles Bar, founded in 1868 has a fine collection of art as well as a noted collection of locally produced drinks

 Concert in the First Presbyterian Church in Rosemary Street

The rose window in St Peter's Cathedral

 St Peter's Cathedral

Interior of the Ulster Hall

 View over the City to Carrickfergus with St Anne's Cathedral and spire

St Anne's Cathedral

 Ornate marble and memorials inside City Hall

City Hall

The city in the evening looking towards the Falls Road

Queen's University

 Dancers at the Titanic Centre

crepes
crepes
crepes
Coffee
Tea
S.D. Bell's

 Titanic commemoration

Table and settings that should have sai
with the ship, now in the Harbour Off

Murals to the history and culture of Belfast and Northern Ireland, with guide

54 Napoleon's Nose, the rocky outcrop on Cave Hill said to resemble the Emperor's profile

The Albert Memorial Clock and Queen's Square

 One of Belfast's many clocks

The Northern Ireland Assembly buildings at Stormont

 The Gasworks site, much of it saved from destruction by poet Sir John Betjeman

Life-size statue called *The Searcher* outside Holywood Arches Library depicting the Belfast-born author C S Lewis as a character in his novel, *TheChronicles of Narnia*

62 Stained glass in the Harbour Commissioners Office celebrating the maritime past of the City

Ornate glass and decoration in the former Ulster Bank HQ (now a hotel)

Published by Gateway Publishing Ltd, **www.gatewaysark.co.uk**
ISBN 978 1 902471112
Photographs by Chris Andrews
Introductory text by Barry Flynn. Captions by Raymond O'Regan and Chris Andrews
Edited by Derek Gallop
Distribution by Gateway Publishing Ltd and
Chris Andrews Publications Ltd, 15 Curtis Yard, North Hinksey Lane, Oxford, OX2 0LX
Tel +44(0)1865 723404 **www.cap-ox.com** enquiries@cap-ox.com

Front Cover: City Hall at dusk Back Cover: Titanic Quarter at dawn and *A Hundred Thousand Welcomes*
Title page: SS Nomadic

H & W